without you

without you
Surviving After Her Death

a sequel to losing you

GEORGE SIMON

TATE PUBLISHING
AND ENTERPRISES, LLC

Published by Tate Publishing & Enterprises, LLC
127 E. Trade Center Terrace | Mustang, Oklahoma 73064 USA
1.888.361.9473 | www.tatepublishing.com

Tate Publishing is committed to excellence in the publishing industry. The company reflects the philosophy established by the founders, based on Psalm 68:11,
"The Lord gave the word and great was the company of those who published it."

Published in the United States of America

ISBN: 978-1-62902-058-7
13.12.13

To all those who have suffered the loss of a loved one, especially the loss of a spouse due to cancer.

Thanks

I want to thank my sisters, Sharon, Jackie and Sue for being the sounding board for both *Losing You* and *Without You*. Their help in these projects cannot be overstated. I am eternally grateful.

Foreword

Writing a personal story let alone one that is about the death of your wife cannot but be excruciatingly difficult and require a critical discipline to overcome the pain that comes with each written word. Your fingers burn, your heart aches and yet you are compelled to go on because it is the only way you can cope and share a love story about the person you miss so terribly.

❧

Without You, by George Simon is more than a terribly tragic event in one man's life but an intimate look into the ravages of pancreatic cancer and the effect it had on George, his dear family, friends and close knit community that surrounded him.

❧

The book gives the reader a chance to feel and share a love story without feeling like an intrusive participant. The frustration and pain oozes out of the pages to reveal that in the end we are all mortal and that there is nothing we can do to stop the inevitable no matter how much intervention, pleading or bargaining we make. You find yourself wanting to scream at the pages …no…no…It can't be! I wanted to get on my knees and pray to God for one more miracle.

❧

Aside from the ravages of Mary Ann's struggle with cancer there is more to be learned in Without You. From it we can see that hope does endure and that while happiness may be fleeting, love is boundless and saying "till death do us part" are more than mere words on a page said a long time ago. We also learn about the practical reality of balancing an unbelievable difficult situation and keeping up with the day to day requirements that allows a family to keep running. After all, bills still need to be paid, the grass has to be mowed and there are still birthdays to be attended to.

❧

Cancer, or any major health care crisis for that matter, plays havoc on the affected family. George and his family are no less taxed physically or emotionally, notwithstanding the crushing financial burdens needed to keep Mary Ann in as comfortable a place as possible and affording her every opportunity to get better. The entire weight of all of that sat squarely on George's shoulders. But that was never the primary concern of

George or even his family. No stone was left unturned or any possible modality of success not looked at. Failure was not an option.

꧂

The true and unspoken dark side for those family members facing the challenges of a devastating and intractable disease is its ever present foreboding force that increasingly weaves its insidious tentacles with each passing day. As time passes, the panic and desperation becomes more palpable and yet there is no choice but to fight on against the rage and frustration. A twig in hurricane force winds. George has to put his best face on each day, not only for Mary Ann but for everyone else, too. To be positive, to lead the cheering, to be the face of hope. George and his family have to learn how to treat Mary Ann's cancer like an unwelcomed guest with all the danger of a thief in the night that you know is there but you can't do much to get rid of.

꧂

As the family gathered to say goodbye to Mary Ann she gives George one final gift for their love and shared life. Mary Ann sheds a last tear at her end. It is a metaphor for their happiness and sadness. The happiness for their life together and the sadness that they will be apart. As George rested his head on her one last time and said "I

11

love you," he knew he had to let her go that day but not forever. Their faith gives George comfort to know that Mary Ann is waiting for him and will sit beside him one more time to hold his hand in hers.

George did not write this book so the reader would feel sorry for him but to honor the memory of the love of his life that he cannot bear to be without and help other grieving families who have gone through this process and those who yet have to go down this road. For that I am thankful and we are all better for it.

In the end, all we are left with are the memories to savior and cherish. This is a story that will stay with you and hopefully remind you when you think about it, to hug and hold those you love a little harder and a little closer.

—Carlo Koren

Prologue

Without hearing her laugh. Without smelling the scent of her favorite perfume. Without hearing the latest story from school. Without hearing her say I love you. Without seeing her each day at supper. Without holding or kissing her. Being without her is to be without life and life has no meaning without her.

❧

My beautiful wife has been gone since July 7, 2012. It has been a time filled with grief, emotional upheaval, and hardship, not only for me personally, but for my family as well as we all try to make sense of our loss and try to cope with our grief and move on. Mary Ann was the center of our universe, and her passing has left us with an incredible void in our lives, in our day-to-day interactions with each other and with others outside of our family. It has been a roller coaster of emotions from depression, to hate for the disease that took her, to joy in knowing that she is in heaven and free of pain, and then back again.

꧁

My family will never accept her loss, but in time, we will learn to live with it, as much as that is possible. This is our story, but it is also her story and the story of anyone who has lost someone who means the world to them.

The Beginning

It was a hot June night in 1970—a Friday night, to be exact. Two of my friends and I decided to go bar hopping with the goal of meeting girls. We had been to several places when we arrived at the Mad Hatter, a disco bar in downtown Cleveland, Ohio with a lighted dance floor. I really didn't like to dance, and neither did my two friends, but this place looked very promising from the girl standpoint. The Mad Hatter was the kind of dance place that was packed all the time—the kind of packed that allowed you go into the crowd and move from one side of the room to the other without your feet ever touching the floor.

꘎

We went in and around the wall that separated the dance floor from the front door. Almost immediately, I saw her sitting at a table about halfway down on the left side of the room. She was with two of her friends, and she was stunningly beautiful! She had long blond hair that fell over her shoulders and reached halfway down her back. Her eyes were a brilliant blue that sparkled in the light of the dance floor. She had the most incredible smile I had ever seen. Simply put, she was the most beautiful girl I had ever seen. Who could blame me for falling in love with her? She was wearing yellow short shorts that revealed her long silky legs. She was very tall, almost as tall as I, who stood six feet.

❧

I had to meet her, and even though I am a shy person, I mustered the courage to walk over and ask her to dance. To my surprise and great joy, she agreed. We danced most of the rest of the night, and I discouraged others who came over to ask for a dance with a look that said, *She's mine. Back off.* Once, when she went to the restroom, I spoke to one of her friends, who was even taller than her. She told me that they had come from a John Carroll University bar where Mary Ann had won the Best Legs Contest. I told you she was beautiful!

❧

I fell in love with her that night—deeply in love. I know it sounds crazy, but it's true, it truly was love at first sight. I fell in love with her right then and there, and that love is still with me today. I was able to get her to give me her telephone number, and all the way home, I worried that she had given me a fake number. I had asked her if she would like to go out with me the next day, and she had said yes, but I was still worried about the number.

On the way home with my two friends, I told them that I had just met the girl I was going to marry. They both laughed, but I knew she was the one. Now I had to make her realize that I was the one for her. It was an exciting beginning!

The First Date

The next day, I called her and asked her to go see a movie with me, and then we would get a burger at a place in North Royalton. She told me the night before that she loved big gooey burgers and The Shake Shoppe made the biggest and best gooey burger in Cleveland. She had never been there. We decided to eat first and so went to The Shake Shoppe.

❧

This place had been there for a long time and was family run. There were no sit down seats, you had to park and order from the counter in front of the place. My friend that was with me when I met Mary Ann and I used to run to The Shake Shoppe and back from our house in Parma, a distance of around eight miles one way, to get ready for football when we were in high school. I ordered two Big Bears, the name of the biggest burger and named after the high school sports teams. We were parked on the side of the shop with several other cars. She loved the burger and finished before me. We talked about what we were doing with our lives. She was enrolled in a Catholic girls' college that produced only teachers and nurses. She would start her junior year in the fall, majoring in education, and I told her I was attending Cleveland State, majoring in business and psychology with a minor in German.

※

When it was time to leave, I packed all of the garbage in the bags the food came in and took it to one of the garbage cans provided by The Shake Shoppe that sat in front of my car. I got back in the car but couldn't find my keys. I looked everywhere—on the floor, in all my pockets, under the seat, even on the ground under the car, everywhere. I apologized for losing them telling her I had never lost them before. It was embarrassing. Our first date and I was looking like some kind of idiot! She suggested that I might have thrown them away with the garbage. I thought she might be right, so I got out of the car and took off the top of the garbage can and started to pull out the garbage piece by piece. Carefully, I looked through each piece of garbage, searching for the keys before I threw it on the ground. I could see that the occupants in the other parked cars nearby found my plight quite funny while Mary Ann had a serious but concerned look on her face. The garbage was piled up around me and I had emptied the can. Still no keys! Now it was time to panic! I looked at her with what must have been a bewildered look and saw her sitting there with a big smile, holding up the keys! She had them all the time! She had watched as I made a fool of myself in front of perfect strangers! When I got in the car, all she said was, "I wanted to see if you had a sense of humor." I thought about that a second and thought humor must be important to her. I laughed, but I knew to look out for her as she was a real practical joker. Then we left for the movie.

I Got You, Babe

As our relationship grew, so did our love for each other, and so did her love of the practical joke. One of her favorites was to have me go in a store to pay a bill, and she would move the car so that when I came out I didn't know where she was. I started taking the keys with me but that didn't work as she had her own set of keys. Even when we had kids she continued to move the car and they thought it was funny to see me wander around the parking lot looking for them.

❧

Her practical jokes didn't stop with me, they extended to school where she was responsible for many of the jokes played on the staff. One such joke was the time she got some St. Joe's letter head and typed a note to one of the male teachers from the pastor of the church, indicating that he wanted to speak to him about some performance issue. She put it in his mail box in the office. All day he sweated and worried about what he had done and what the pastor wanted to see him for. He called the pastor's office in the afternoon after worrying himself almost to death and asked for the pastor. When the pastor came on the phone the teacher asked what he wanted to talk to him about. He was told that he did not want to talk to him at all. As soon as the pastor told him that, he knew that Mary Ann had struck again. Later he blamed the incident for a slight heart attack he had. No one ever knew if that was true but it did seem plausible.

※

Our friends likened us to Sonny & Cher, a popular rock couple and TV personalities of the time. Cher was constantly making Sonny the butt of her jokes, just as Mary Ann did with me. In fact, at one faculty party, everyone sang a song and ours was "I Got You Babe" by Sonny & Cher…. Mary Ann picked it out.

※

Mary Ann graduated in 1972 and found a job teaching at the Catholic elementary school she attended as a child. It was much later that she worked at the Sts. Joseph & John School. In between, we were married on June 15, 1974. Both of the guys who were with me when I met her were in our wedding party. Who's laughing now? When we had our first child in 1978, we decided she would stay home until the youngest was in first grade. We always talked about having four kids. I had four in my family and so did Mary Ann. Our four children were almost two years apart. When we told her parents she was pregnant with our fourth, her mother said that every time I came home from the Army Mary Ann got pregnant. I reminded her that she had four children but she said, "That was different." She stayed home for almost twelve years. Those years were happy years. She was always with the kids, taking them to all the places young mothers take their children—T ball, soccer, the zoo, dance lessons, swim lessons, everywhere and anywhere she wanted. I was traveling on business or with the Army, but I still helped her as much as I could. We shared the house work, Mary Ann never had to do all the work and still work outside the home. I did the sweeping and washing of floors, windows and bathrooms. She did the dusting, cooking and washed clothes. I also did all the yard work. We shared the work. I didn't want her to stand the burden of raising the kids and have to do all the house work.

❧

When I was away with the Army she had to fill in. She would wash my uniforms when I had field problems. I was not allergic to anything like Poison Ivy but she was and sometimes she got it just by handling the uniforms. Revenge for all of the practical jokes was sweet! I was almost always home for the weekends. We were content, we were satisfied with our life together, we loved our family, and we made plans for the future. One of the songs she liked was "When I'm Sixty-Four" by the Beatles. It was hard to imagine us being sixty-four when we were in the prime of our life, but we talked frequently about what it might be like, growing old together—a goal that would never be achieved.

☙

Time passed. The kids grew up, and our lives took on a new phase. We were thinking about each other more and doing things more for us now. The kids were either in college or high school, and we were looking forward to being empty nesters, a time that would mimic the years when we were first married or so we thought. It happened subtly—at first only on weekends, then as time went on and the kids were married or had moved out to be on their own, we found ourselves alone. We were terrified of this rediscovered freedom. We, and especially Mary Ann, were still in family activity planning mode. The trouble was there was no one to plan for or even if there was one or two, they didn't want us to plan for them. She had a hard time planning meals as all the meals she had been making were for six, and now there were only two of us. She never knew if anyone would show up for supper so she usually made enough for four. If she thought we might not have enough, she would always tell me not to eat much so the kids could have enough.

❧

During this time period Becky was married and lived in Brunswick with Gerry, her husband. Sara was attending Kent State University and was getting serious with someone she met there, and I swore Greg into the Army. Matt was going to school and working in Columbus, Ohio.

❧

She immersed herself in her school work and volunteered for almost all extra school activities. She was especially good at collecting money and clothing for the poor and I remember many years that at the end of the clothing drive she had several thousand T shirts in her room at school. Shirts and sometimes tennis shoes or coats were also collected. One year she also collected blankets and had several hundred of those to give to the poor. Her kids would always help in counting the clothes; they folded them and placed them in boxes ready for pick up by the charity she contacted. When our son, Greg was in Afghanistan she organized a Christmas tree drive for the troops who would spend the holiday away from home. She talked a craft store into donating several hundred plastic Christmas trees about two feet high. The kids in her classes made ornaments and wrote cards to the soldiers. She then got several businesses to send the trees to troops in Afghanistan addressed only to any American soldier. She was a miracle worker. On most nights, she arrived home about six fifteen in the evening, but some nights it was later. She left for school at six ten every day. I continued to travel for work. We may have had the freedom of earlier years but you'd never know it. We had more money, but again, you would not know it. All our energy was channeled into work and the kids, who thought they were independent, but were still dependent on us for many things.

❧

Usually, by the weekends, we were too tired to do much of anything. It seemed as though we were alone together but not together as we had thought. That Sonny & Cher song still played in my head: "Put your little hand in mine, / there ain't no hill or mountain we can't climb / I got you babe.

If Life Is a Bowl of Cherries, How Did We Get the Pits?

Time marched on. Mary Ann and I were still very much in love, but our lives had changed, and we both saw the change coming. She never had a sister so she wanted to be as close to her daughters as possible and since both were living in town, we spent most of our free time going between them. Sara graduated from Kent State, was married and preparing to move to Virginia with her husband who also graduated from Kent State and had secured a job teaching in a school district there. Becky lived in her own home with her husband and was close enough that we could walk there with our Golden Retriever, Harry. We also went to see Mary Ann's mother every weekend. Sometimes it got crazy, but she always managed to work things out. Life was fast paced. In fact, I thought it was much faster than when the kids were small.

❧

In April of 2010, our younger daughter and her husband had their first baby. Mary Ann was thrilled! She was just as thrilled as when we had our first. I have a photo of Mary Ann holding our first and another of her holding her first grandchild. The expression on her face is the same—that of complete joy. Up to that point, we had babysat only the family dogs, whom we loved dearly; but it was different now with a grandchild. We didn't know it, but even then, she had the pancreatic cancer tumor growing for almost a year in her, and sometime in late 2010 or early 2011, it spread to her liver. No symptoms, nothing to warn us of this monster growing within her. In her world, all was well; and with the birth of our grandchild, all was perfect.

❧

In December of 2010, I interviewed and was offered a position with a Workers' Compensation company in Louisiana. I discussed whether I should take it because I knew that she had at least two years, 2011 and 2012, to work before she could get full retirement benefits. I had thought that it may be too long to be away, even if I came home once a month. She assured me that I was the only one for her and that I should take the job. I guess I just wanted her assurance that she still loved me and it would be okay to go that far away for such long periods. I did take the position, and I started on January 17, 2011. I called her at least once a day, and we also had Skype on our laptops so we could see each other, which made both of us feel like we were there with the other. Still the joker, sometimes when we turned Skype on, she had Harry sitting on the chair looking into the screen with her voice. One time when Skype came on, she was turned around so I could not see her face and when she did turn around, she had one of those green face masks that women use, with big rollers in her hair. She just wanted to see what I would say. I told her how beautiful she looked that night. She was always the joker.

❧

My boss was very understanding and gave me one free day a month to go home. Things seemed to be going well both at work and at home. Then Mary Ann had a mini stroke and several weeks later felt pain in her back and under the right rib cage. After tests were completed, she was diagnosed with stage 4 pancreatic and liver cancer. This devastating news changed our lives forever. When I knew that her condition was becoming worse, I went home and worked from home so that I could be with her. This allowed me to continue working without taking a medical leave, while at the same time be with and help my wife. Again, my boss was very understanding and encouraged me to go home sooner than I had planned.

⚜

Before I went home, my son Matt was taking care of her. I had asked him to quit his job in Columbus, Ohio and come home to help his mother the day after she was diagnosed. I needed someone who we could count on, someone steady and dependable; that was Matt. I felt guilty about that and asked her many times if I could come home, but she always said, "When the time is right." By April 2012, it was. I didn't ask her if I could come home, I told her I was coming home. She didn't say anything, she knew it was time.

⚜

The cancer was the worst thing that could have happened, to her and to our family. Mary Ann was the rock of the family and the center of our universe. The diagnosis totally devastated her and all of us. In an instant all of our lives, our hopes and dreams were changed forever. I thought about our life and how it had been, up to that point, a bowl of cherries; but this disease changed everything. Now we had the pits.

The Battle of Forevermore

Mary Ann had stage 4 pancreatic and liver cancer, the kind that only 5 percent of people afflicted with it ever recover from. That 5 percent usually had the cancer diagnosed early, before it could spread to other organs. It was discovered because of some other condition such as stomach problems and tests on the stomach showed the pancreatic tumor. Mary Ann was not that lucky. Her cancer had already spread from the pancreas to the liver. She did have an occasional back pain but, she had them since I had first known her. I thought she had picked up something with her back, not her legs as she should have. I told her many times over the course of years about using her legs when she lifts things. We simply had no clue about the cancer. She was initially given six months or less to live by a large clinic in Cleveland who would not treat her. That forced us to go out of network. They told us, "There is nothing we could offer." But, we got a second opinion from University Hospital's Seidman Cancer Center who gave us four treatment options and we embarked on the most aggressive treatment program that extended her life for fourteen months after diagnosis. We could never repay the Seidman doctors and staff for their kindness, caring approach and professionalism shown to Mary Ann and me during her treatment. They made us feel like family; I will never forget them.

※

Fourteen months of life, but of pure hell for her and for us as well. Fourteen months of having to watch the one you love so much, suffer unspeakable pain, suffer through long periods of nausea, diarrhea, body sores including in the mouth, watch as she lost so much weight that she actually looked like a walking skeleton—something from a concentration camp. I could put my index finger and thumb around her thigh, and what was most upsetting to her, watch as her beautiful hair fell out. But, I would never give back one second of those fourteen months. Their efforts allowed Mary Ann to live more than twice as long as the other clinic had predicted and they showed us how truly caring health care practitioners can be.

※

The worry that comes with a diagnosis like this affects everyone in the family. You could see it in their faces, hear it in their voices; depressed and worried for their mother. Would the treatments work? Every time there was a CT scan there was the worry that it would show the tumors receding or show them growing or that the cancer had moved to some other organ. Every pain she had made you think that the treatment was not working or that the cancer had moved somewhere else. Would she be able to take the chemo or would she have to stop it? What other treatments might be available if the chemo stops? Would she be able to eat enough to maintain her strength? The worry never stopped, and in fact, as time passed and I could see the effects of the cancer and the treatment, it actually increased the worry. She became so weak, so fragile that it seemed that she was one step away from death for months. I witnessed a beautiful vibrant woman, my wife, regress from a youthful energetic person to an old sick and dying woman and I could do nothing to help her. I saw this and could not tell if it was a result of the cancer, the treatments or both, that so racked her body.

❧

It leaves the family of the cancer victim feeling powerless, helpless and depressed as they watch a loved one battling to save their life; but, as an observer, you realize that your loved one will not survive and there is *nothing* that you can do to save them. *Nothing* … except to pray. You can't sleep, your appetite is nonexistent. While the loved one battles the cancer, you battle depression; but you must put on your best face for your family and for your loved one every day. You can never let your loved one know your true thoughts. You do your best to hide the worry that eats at you daily, and you never stop telling her that you love her, no matter what the medical news is. This is what living with Cancer is like for the family. I cannot imagine what it is like for the victim.

✌

Mary Ann never quit fighting the disease. She always thought that she would somehow, some way beat this cancer, and for some time it looked like she might. We all prayed that she would. Besides her family, she had hundreds of people praying for her. Even at the end, when she had only hours of life left, her blood pressure suddenly went up instead of down as the doctor had told us it would. She was still fighting it. She was joined in this battle by her family, her school, her friends, and by the community of Strongsville, where she taught for twenty years and was so well loved. Former students who had grown up, married, had families and moved out of the city and sometimes out of state, came to see her and prayed for her. The teachers at her school prayed for her and organized four fund raisers at different restaurants and each was a sellout. Each classroom at school prayed for her every day.

❧

Her students were very protective of her at school; even those who were in the eighth grade came to see her every morning to cheer her up. Her students respected her, as well. She didn't have any kids who misbehaved when she was out of the room. They knew what was happening to her, and they did everything they could to help her. Most of these kids came to the funeral to say their final good-byes to a teacher they loved and respected. Some were on vacation and could not attend. Some wrote on her CaringBridge site, some made videos for her to watch, some walked to our house to visit her in the summer, and one even nominated her for the Crystal Apple Award for educational excellence, which she received near the end of her last year. Her kids at school protected her; they helped her and empowered her with the will to keep on fighting the cancer. They did this because they loved her and respected her. There is no doubt in my mind that her kids played a major part in her success in the treatment program and in the length and quality of life during her journey.

❧

Even while all the hideous things were happening to her, Mary Ann taught full time, and she taught all year, ending in June 2012, just four weeks before she died. No one thought she could teach that long; nor did they think she would finish the year, but she was a fighter, and nothing was going to stop her from doing what she loved so much. She actually signed her contract for the next year that the principal brought to our house after school was over. She knew that Mary Ann would never teach again but this kind act meant so much to Mary Ann. She was so excited and convinced that she would teach again that when the principal left she started looking through her lesson planner, getting ready for the next year. This was three weeks before she died.

❧

She was the English and religion teacher for seventh grade at Sts. Joseph & John School in Strongsville. Her faith was rock solid, unshakable. We never once heard her complain about why she had this disease, why these terrible things were happening to her. She never questioned God about the cancer, or the horrible pain that woke her at night, or the nausea or diarrhea, or the loss of weight, or her hair falling out. No, she accepted her cross and was determined to make the best of this, her fate. My daughter Becky said that "Mom was given lemons and she made lemonade." Mary Ann once told me that no one ever knows what will be handed them in life but if you trust in God then you must accept His plan. She did.

❧

During the last year of her life, she had several religious experiences involving the Blessed Mother, Saint Theresa, and Jesus. These experiences helped her cope; they helped her accept what was happening to her; they reinforced her belief in God, her Catholic faith, and her will to fight on, which she did right to the end. Her will to live was remarkable. Her never-give-up attitude not only empowered her but it gave all of us who loved her the will to keep supporting her battle to the end, and we did. I truly believe that her faith helped to prolong her life. It gave added meaning to her life. It was a source of comfort to her and to us. Faith and the promise of eternal life is what it is all about.

❧

Mary Ann gave it her all and then some. We who were with her on her journey were in awe of her, of her fortitude, of her sheer strength in body, mind and spirit. In the end, she could not will herself to be made whole, and neither could we. During her journey, her blood cancer number went from almost one million when she was diagnosed to just over three hundred, close to normal.

※

She told me the night before we left on vacation that she had accepted the will of God. That was the first and only time that she acknowledged to me that she would not win her battle with cancer. As I had done every day since she got out of school, I asked her if she wanted to go on vacation or stay home with me and the dogs. I told her that I would be happy to stay home with her and that we would have time to be alone together. Again, she said she wanted to go. I was not going to tell her she couldn't. I kissed her, hugged her and told her I loved her more than anything in my life. I hoped that she would live long enough to enjoy the vacation with the kids and grandkids. That was not to be.

※

She died on July 7, 2012 at 1:43 a.m. on a Saturday morning. One of her students wrote that the time was significant because it meant "I love you." *I* has one letter, *Love* has four, and *You* has three. I always thought that this was what she was trying to tell me just before she closed her eyes and died. Mary Ann could not talk during the hours before her death. Just before she died she opened her eyes, looked at me and cried. She couldn't speak. I asked, "Honey, why are you crying? Everything is okay." And I hugged her and kissed her, telling her how much I loved her as I dabbed the tears. Then she closed her eyes and was gone, gone forevermore.

The Funeral

Mary Ann passed into eternity in the early morning hours of July 7, 2012, at 1:43 a.m. I was with her as I had been since I came home to care for her in April. My sister from Cincinnati, who had recently lost her husband, was with me at Mary Ann's bedside. She was a great comfort to me, but I don't know how she could deal with the loss of two loved ones so close together.

❧

I remember watching my wife as she lay in bed after her death. She looked as if she was just sleeping. She looked peaceful now, calm. Her ordeal was over; the pain was gone forever. Every so often, I would get up from the chair and hug and kiss her and tell her I loved her. But I knew she didn't hear me; she would never respond to me again. She lay there almost serene, but I was tormented by her passing, a passing made worse by having to watch the one I loved so much suffer the final indignities of this disease and not being able to do anything to stop it.

❧

I was so very tired; I hadn't slept in the last four days. I never left her side, not even to sleep. I had to be near her in case she awoke and needed me. Now she had left me, but not forever, as I know that I will be with her again; when that time comes, it will be forever. For now, I knew that she had gone home,… that's all,… gone home to God.

❧

I couldn't watch her being taken away, and my sister took me home at four am. We would need to plan the funeral, and she helped me with that as well. The afternoon of July 7, she and I met the funeral director to choose a casket for Mary Ann—a beautiful white one with gold handles and a light-pink interior. It had a drawer in it where we could put our letters to Mary Ann, our private thoughts and remembrances. The kids each wrote their own letter to her. I wrote about our life together and told her again that I was the luckiest man alive to have shared in her life, that I loved her from the first moment I saw her and that I would always love her and that we would be together again, forever.

❧

We were told that we needed to bring clothes and whatever jewelry we wanted her to wear. I picked out a royal blue dress I had gotten for her to wear on our thirty-eighth wedding anniversary on June 15, and a gold necklace with a cluster of diamonds and sapphires in the center, along with diamond-studded earrings. She would wear her most comfortable black shoes. She made me promise that I would not bury her with the diamond rings. She wanted the girls to have them. All she wanted was the wedding band and her mother's ring with the birthstone of each of her children. I made sure that her wishes were carried out.

❧

My sister and daughters helped me find everything, and we took them to the funeral home. Mary Ann would be laid out for two days and buried the third day after the funeral mass at St. Joseph Church next to the school where she had taught for twenty years. I was still so very tired; my mind was a blur for everything except that which had to do with Mary Ann. I wanted to make her funeral special; I wanted her to know how much everyone loved her, how much I loved her and always would. I remember all of it. It is burned into my mind, and I can recall and see things as though they are still happening.

❧

We arrived for the first viewing early. The director told me that he lived in Strongsville and he knew from talking with neighbors that there would be a lot of people there. In fact, I was told later that it was one of the largest funerals in Strongsville's history. There were nearly eight hundred people who came to see Mary Ann the first day, and almost five hundred the second. The procession to the church had over sixty cars in it. The mayor of Strongsville gave Mary Ann a motorcycle escort from the funeral home to the church and then to the cemetery. He had known Mary Ann for many years. She had met him while food shopping Friday evenings. He was there with his elderly father. This was his way of saluting her. They had to coordinate with three other cities for the funeral caravan to pass through. She was much loved.

ॐ

I remember that I was very emotional. I am not usually an emotional man, but that day, I could not stop crying. So it was with my family and most everyone who came to see her. I remember standing in line a very long time, thanking people who came and accepting condolences; but the strange thing is I don't remember many of the faces. I remember figures, but not faces. Mary Ann's ninety-two-year-old mother was brought in to see her, and she would not accept that she was looking at her daughter. She kept saying, "That's not my Mary Ann". I think my whole family felt the same. We could not believe that she was gone. The second day was a shorter viewing, but again, there were so many who came to see her that it took a long time for them to go through the line leading to the casket.

❦

Throughout the viewing, a CD's worth of pictures of Mary Ann and our family that spanned the years played on several monitors around the room. My daughters made several large picture posters of the significant phases of Mary Ann's life—her childhood, her teen years, our wedding, our family, and her teaching years. She had won the Crystal Apple Award her last year, an Oscar for teaching, and we displayed the Crystal Apple. A beautiful picture of her taken for her college graduation that was also used for the engagement announcement and which now hangs in my office, was displayed near the head of the casket.

❦

There were so many flower arrangements from close friends, relatives, and people I don't know that went down both sides of the room and across the back. I asked the director to give the flowers that didn't go to the cemetery to the retirement homes in Strongsville, in her name. He called later to tell me all flowers were delivered and it took several van loads to deliver all of them. I asked my son Greg to wear his dress blue uniform for the day of the funeral, as Mary Ann always said she loved the way he looked in it. My boss, Geoff, came up from Louisiana for the funeral.

I was going to give the eulogy, but Father Bob convinced me that it would be better if he did, as I would be too emotional. He was right, and I am very grateful for his advice. The eulogy he delivered was outstanding. Father Bob grew up very close to Mary Ann's house and frequently played with her older brothers. I wish she could have heard his descriptions of her life. I sat with my sons and daughters and their spouses in the first row. I can't tell you how seeing the casket wheeled up the main isle of the church tore our hearts out. It was gut wrenching seeing her casket and knowing that soon she would be gone from our sight forever. It was all sinking in now; she was gone. I really don't remember much of the Mass other than it seemed to pass quickly. I was too busy praying for Mary Ann and crying. Every time I looked at my family, I would see them wiping away tears. My own handkerchief was soaked before the Mass ended. I would relive this event every day of my life

The procession came out of the church and proceeded to the Holy Cross Cemetery, to the plot I had recently purchased for Mary Ann and me. I did not tell her that I had bought it as I did not want her to be upset or to know that she would not survive the disease. She never asked about a plot, I never mentioned it either. I was lucky enough to get a spot seven plots away from her father's grave and where her mother will be buried. The pallbearers placed her coffin on the stand, and Father Bob read the final prayers and then concluded the funeral. I placed a white carnation on her casket and kissed the lid, saying my last good-bye to the one love of my life. I had known her for forty-two years, and we were married for thirty-eight—too short of a time to be together.

It was over; the long ordeal was finally over for her, but it will never be over for me or, for that matter, for my family. The funeral was ended. As I walked away, I thought that so too was my life ended; and now came the hard part—living without her.

Making Sense of It

My daughter, Becky and Gerry, my son-in-law, took me home from the cemetery. I have little recollection of the events after the funeral. My head was still spinning from her death on Saturday, and the lack of sleep combined to blur the events after her death. There was a lunch at the church for anyone who was at the funeral. I spoke at that gathering, but to this day, I do not recall what I said; at least I don't recall most of it. I know others also spoke about Mary Ann, but again, I do not remember much of what was said or by whom. I was pretty much burned out, cried out, and running on sheer willpower.

❧

We arrived at our house with a few close relatives. A home now empty of the person for whom it had existed, for which it had been built, lovingly furnished, and cared for. *Empty.* Such a word described how I felt, how the kids felt, and how we saw the house now. Rommel and Harry, our German Shepherd and Golden Retriever, were glad as usual to see us but could sense there was something different today. Rommel went from room to room looking for Mary Ann, the person he loved and protected. Harry too seemed to count heads as if he also recognized someone was not there.

❧

I told everyone that I had to lie down; I excused myself and went to our bedroom. When I walked in the room the emptiness hit me. I would never see her in this room again, never touch her, never kiss her, never make love to the woman I swore to love, honor and cherish all my life. I hated this room now. I hated what it now stood for and the emptiness it conveyed. All around were reminders of her, reminders of our life together. Now they stood alone, silent reminders of a life now gone, reminders that will stare at me every time I come into this room.

❧

Here was her dressing table that I bought for her on a business trip to North Carolina. It had pictures in frames standing on it and had others hanging from the wall next to it. Mary Ann loved the dressing table. It was her connection to her femininity, her womanhood. And over on the opposite wall was her dresser with the statue of the Guardian Angel, with kids walking over a bridge. She loved it so much. Next to it was her mirror, brush-and-comb set that she said was for show only as it was too good to use. Her chifferobe with a mirror was loaded with pictures on top, and every drawer was full of her sweaters. She allowed me to have one drawer in the high dresser. All the rest were hers, and she had more than enough clothes to fill them and the walk-in closet. There were so many pictures, many with her in them. All seemed to be staring at me. This was a very lonely room now. I lay on her side of the bed and fell into a deep sleep. Maybe this was a bad dream that will be over when I wake up.

%

Becky and her husband, Gerry, stayed for a few more days. She wanted to help sort through her mother's clothes, and I asked her to look at Mary Ann's jewelry to see if there was anything she wanted. Mary Ann had many expensive pieces, and I wanted them to be shared between her and Sara. I saved some for Amy, my daughter-in-law.

%

This was a hard task for Becky. She had tried so hard to help Mary Ann beat the cancer. She too was drained from the long ordeal and had to stop as it was too much for her to do so soon after her mother's passing. Normally, I would not have asked her to look through her mother's things, but I knew she would be returning to New Jersey soon and would not be back for a long while. Becky deeply felt the pain of the loss of her mother, and her usually lighthearted personality gave way to uncharacteristic silence.

※

Matt was not as emotional as I was, but he was affected by his mother's passing. He had spent so much time caring for his mother that now there was a sense of relief that it was over, but at the same time, there was a sense of loss that he felt deeply. He went to some close friend's house later that day and stayed the night.

※

Greg showed very little emotion during the days in the funeral home or at the cemetery. Perhaps three tours in war zones were to blame, or maybe it was the fact that he was on a military funeral detail and helped bury many young soldiers. I don't know for sure. I was worried about him, but I reminded myself that he rarely wore his emotions on his sleeve.

※

Sara was very emotional. She was with Mary Ann almost every day, and although she knew that Mary Ann would not be successful in her fight, she always held out that there was hope, as Mary Ann did. I think that sometimes when this happens, the outcome, as bad as it is, is still not anticipated and comes as a shock. Sara was shocked at her mother's passing, and her emotional demeanor showed that. Her mother was gone, and she deeply felt the pain of loss. She was aided by her husband, Mike, and their daughter, Ava. We all talked about the struggle and the outcome, but no one could make sense of it. I don't think anyone ever will.

Simon & Garfunkel's song "Bookends Lyric Theme" summed up all my feelings of that room.

> Time it was, and what a time it was, it was
> A time of innocence, a time of confidences
> Long ago, it must be, I have a photograph
> Preserve your memories; they're all that's left you.

I realized that this room, the room that, more than any other symbolized the love between a man and woman, the heart of the house, had now grown cold.

What Now

Several weeks passed with little being done by anyone. I thought that this must be how it is when someone dies that meant so much to you, to the family. Everyone is walking around in some kind of funk. The shock of the death still lingers, and everyone seems in a daze, disjointed, and lacking any direction. No one knows what to say, and even when the kids visit, there is very little by way of conversations. I certainly felt this way, and so too did my family. As I thought about my new life without her, I realized that life in the rest of the world had moved on. The big question I had was, *What do I do now?*

꽃

Mary Ann was a great organizer. Everything had a place, and she always made sure that things ran smoothly. The last few months were very different. She was not able to run the house as she had always done. Matt and I did the cooking and cleaning, but she who had always handled the money could not do that anymore. She suffered from chemo brain and could not remember bank accounts, passwords, or identification codes for the accounts that the bills were paid through, and which bills were paid either at stores or through the mail. Luckily, she had arranged for some bills, such as the house payment, to be on auto pay, so at least we were never behind on these, because there were many that were not paid on time. As I looked for bills, I found that she basically quit paying them near the end of April, and it was now late July. Although I had gotten her a rolltop desk and wooden drawers for taking care of money and other matters, including schoolwork, after April, she could not remember to even put the bills in the proper folders. I found most of them on the desk, in the desk, on the top of the drawers, on the desk chair, and in some drawers. There were stacks of bills dating April through the end of July, along with some dated early August.

❧

I was depressed. I was not willing to accept her death, but I saw the bills and knew that no matter how I felt, I had to put that problem as my first priority. I disregarded all April, May, and June bills and called all the providers, stores, and credit card companies to tell them about Mary Ann, and paid as many as I could at the time of the call. Some required payment through the mail. I also set up auto pay with as many as I could, which helped eliminate any potential mistake of not paying bills in the following months. Along with paying bills, something I had never done as Mary Ann wanted complete control of finances, I realized that she had a number of bank accounts from which different bills were paid. This was confusing to me, so I decided to consolidate all accounts with one bank. The problem was that I was not named on all of the accounts. I had to contact a probate attorney to file a motion with the court to allow me to access those accounts in order to consolidate them into one account; it was a timely and costly endeavor. To make matters worse, I had to go back to work in Louisiana in late July, which made coordination of all the bank accounts and bills even more complicated.

※

The fact that I had to get involved in the finances was an eye-opener to me. It made me realize what a great job Mary Ann had done for all those years and what a difficult job it was. Second, having to concentrate on this project helped get me out of the funk that I was in. I would never get over the loss of my wife, but I would move on and hope that the pain of her loss would diminish overtime. The fact that I was busy trying to rectify the bill and bank problem helped me refocus my life, but it did not lessen the pain of her loss. What's next? I would continue on without her because I had to, not because I wanted to. Life would continue, my life had radically and forever changed; and whether or not I wanted it, I was stuck with the prospect of being without her for the rest of my life.

Mary Ann's 2008 Seventh grade photo

Our family 1988

Mary Ann and I at the condo in Myrtle Beach 2006

Mary Ann and I at my sister's house

Mary Ann on our wedding day 1974

Mary Ann 3 weeks before her death at
our 38th wedding anniversary

Mary Ann and I take a train trip during Easter 2012

The Marker

Of the many duties of the surviving spouse, perhaps one of the hardest is purchasing the grave monument. The week after I buried Mary Ann, I went to a local monument company that was located across the street from the cemetery. I had no idea what I wanted or, for that matter, what they cost, but I wanted the very best that I could get for her. I was met by one of the owners of the company, who was very kind and helpful. He asked which cemetery she was in and what the plot number was. I told him that she was across the street but that I didn't remember the plot number. He said that he would find out because each cemetery had rules governing headstones, and most are row specific. For example, if your loved one is in a row where all the stones are ground level, then you may be required to keep your stone at ground level.

※

He made the call and was told that we could have a ground-level stone or one that was raised, which meant that the top edge would be six inches high and the bottom would be three inches, giving the stone a somewhat slanted, upright look. I opted for the slanted look. I wanted her stone to stand out, so I had all the letters and numbers set in twenty-four-carat gold leaf. The stone would be black marble, and the finish would be polished. I took a tour of the facility and picked out a piece that seemed to have already been polished. He indicated that the stone was not yet polished but would be after engraving had been completed.

☙

I wanted her stone to be beautiful, as she was in life. So, too, would her stone be . At the top right would be an engraving of the Blessed Mother, whom she loved, prayed to so much, and was named after. At the top left would be engraved a picture of Jesus. Under the Blessed Mother would be Mary Ann's name, date of birth, and date of death. On the other side would be my name and date of birth. The last name *Simon* would be centered in large letters between the etchings of Mary and Jesus at the top of the stone. Directly in the center between our names and below *Simon* would be a photo of both of us taken at our daughter Becky's wedding. I had a choice of having a computer-generated laser picture made on the stone, or I could to have their artist hand-engrave it at an additional cost. When I compared the laser photographs on stones already completed with the artist's renditions, the artist's work was by far the best choice. Below the picture would be entwined wedding rings with our wedding date and at the bottom, centered, would be the phrase "In Love Forever," which is engraved on both of our wedding rings.

❧

The highly polished black granite would be enhanced by the gold lettering. It would be beautiful. I did not care what the cost was. It was for her, and I always bought her the best of everything. This would be the last thing I would ever buy her—something I never thought I'd have to get.

❧

I was told that the monument would take about six weeks to get ready, which included the cemetery approval of the stone. To my surprise, it was ready in four weeks and placed on her grave in the first week of September.

❧

I visit her every day I am home. I bring a small bench to sit on and talk to her about what's going on in my life, what is new in the family, and about any news that I think she would want to hear. I tell her how sorry I am that I could not save her and how much I love her and miss her. I ask her to wait for me. I ask this every day

I am home with her and every day when I pray for her when I am not home. The marker seems to me to be the hard proof that she is gone; but she will never be out of my life.

The Diary

My daughter Sara called me one evening to tell me that she was going through her mother's drawers in the bedroom and that she found a diary. It was the kind that locks so that only the owner could look at it. It was yellow and covered the years 1972 through our wedding day in 1974, about two years. She said it was a daily account of our courtship and her thoughts about me. I was excited and wanted to know what the general impression was that she had of me as I had never read or remember seeing it. Sara said she only looked at several pages but it was clear that mom was very much in love with me. I asked her to keep the book until I got home so I could see it.

❧

I came home in the middle of October, and Sara brought me the diary. As soon as I saw it I remembered it. I had given it to Mary Ann to record our courtship. This journal was a way she could save the memories of our life before we married. It was very gratifying to read her entries, where she talked about how much she loved me, her impressions of our dates, of the things I bought for her. There were so many things that I had forgotten, and this diary brought all of those memories flooding back to me. Happy times! She reminded me that from the start, she wanted to control the money, and if I disagreed even mildly, she thought we had a fight. I finally wised up and gave in to her by giving her my paychecks, and that ended the only obstacle in our relationship.

※

The journal told about her graduation from college and the worrying she did before she found her first job as a teacher at her Catholic elementary school she attended as a child. You could hear the pride in her voice as she described the first car she ever bought with her own money—a red 1974 Gremlin with black interior. She loved that car. I had forgotten how many times I bought her things just to see her face light up, how many times I took her out to supper or to lunch or just stayed with her at her parents' house. I do remember that once, her father asked her," Doesn't he ever go home?"

※

I read her descriptions of planning for our wedding and how excited she was, and so was I! This journal had done me a wonderful service in renewing my relationship with my wife, reminding me of how much I loved her and how much she loved me and how long we waited to be married. One of the stories it told was when I gave her the engagement ring. Almost always, when I gave her a present, she would look at the box it came in, shake it, and then guess what was inside. To my annoyance, she was almost always right! Once, I gave her a bracelet with animal charms. She shook the box and guessed not only the bracelet but she guessed the animal charms too. When it came time to give her the ring, I decided to wrap it and place it in a box inside of a box, inside of a box with each box being a little smaller than the last. I had at least five boxes with the ring box the last all ready to give to her.

❧

The night arrived, December 21, 1972. I had picked her up from work in Downtown Cleveland, and we were on our way to her mother's house. On the way, I reached in the back and got the large box and handed it to her, telling her that I'd bet my last dollar that she would never guess what it was. She shook the box, turned it upside down, and listened for any noise that would give her a clue as to what was inside. She finally said she didn't know and opened the first box to find another box inside. She pulled it out and shook it, turned it over, listened but could not guess. She opened all of the boxes and came to the ring box. I thought she would guess it at that point, but to my surprise, she held the ring box, performed every test she could think of, but she could not guess what was inside! I had finally stumped her. But did I want to at that point? She opened the box and started to cry and I asked her to marry me, and she said YES!

⚴

I have since read the journal many times, each time finding a new memory that was lost but is now discovered once more. When I read the pages, she lives again, and I hear her voice with each passage, her laughter, and sometimes her disappointment if we had a fight. The diary keeps her alive in my memory. I keep it on the end table next to the couch where I sit in the evenings. It has raised my spirits countless times when the loneliness of my life seems to overpower me. She is alive in this diary, and I hear her voice again recounting the memories— such wonderful memories of our life, of our love and for me, of Mary Ann.

Thanksgiving

I was in Louisiana for about a month before Thanksgiving. I really was not looking forward to this holiday, the first major holiday without her; but being home was better than sitting here alone. I don't mind being here during the week, but I hate weekends when I'm alone and have nothing to do but think of her and wonder why she had to leave me. The hours seem to go so slowly then, and I spend my time thinking about her, about us, and our life together. I wonder, if I had done anything differently, would she still be alive today?

❧

Thanksgiving was one of her favorite days. We always had the family at our house for the meal, and it seemed that as time went on, she had the preparation time down to a science. We would be starting over this year. No one besides Mary Ann had ever made the turkey, or, for that matter, any part of the meal. She always took care of it all. She was a great cook, and all through the morning, our house was filled with the smells of Thanksgiving, the turkey, pumpkin pie, the wonderful stuffing she made.

All of these smells combined to create the symphony of the smells of Thanksgiving. None of that this year.

¥

Matt would be there, as would Greg and his family, along with Sara, Mike, and Ava. Becky and Gerry could not come this year due to work. Of course, Rommel and Harry are always ready to share turkey with us. I arrived home the day before, and Sara and I went to pick out the turkey. We decided we would get a twenty-two-pound bird. Sounds like a big one, but we always got a big turkey, and I wanted this year to be as close to normal as possible. Besides, we always gave everyone some to take home for leftovers or sandwiches. I told Sara that I wanted to eat in the dining room and using the china that Mom always set out. We would set a place for her at the head of the table where she always sat.

¥

I had the turkey in the roaster by 10:30 a.m., and we planned to eat about 2:30 p.m. Sara made the stuffing as Mary Ann had taught her, and it tasted as good. She also made the pie and the other side dishes. Sara is a good cook, as is Becky. Mary Ann had taught them well. Everyone who was coming was at the house and seemed to be in good spirits. The meal was set out, and Sara called everyone to the dining room. This was where the difference began. We were all seated, and Matt had poured wine for all. I stood to give a toast to Mary Ann, who was represented by the empty place setting and chair. I asked everyone to remember their fondest memory of Mom on a Thanksgiving past and to always remember that she is with us. This was where everyone fell silent. From that point on, it was the quietest dinner I have ever been to. Not only was there very little talking, but most of us sat and ate with our heads down. I know Mary Ann would not have wanted that, but I also understood the loss that everyone felt on that special day. Perhaps the toast brought it on, or perhaps it was building up during the day and I didn't see it, I don't know; but everyone at the table felt their loss again, and looking at the empty place was a constant reminder for them.

❧

When dinner was over, the girls cleared the table, and I helped in the kitchen. As I thought about the mood during dinner, I felt it was a mistake to have the empty place even if it was for her. I think she would have been happier to see smiling faces and hear happy conversations than hear the silence in that room. I will not make that mistake at Christmas.

❧

The afternoon drifted into evening, and the kids got ready to go home. We divided what was left of the turkey, and everyone took enough for at least one more meal, which also included stuffing and other side dishes. By 7:00 p.m., everyone had left. I was left at home with my thoughts, my memories of happier Thanksgivings, and, of course, with Rommel and Harry.

Home Alone

One of the worst aspects of becoming a widower is being alone, especially alone the first time after the funeral. For me, that happened on July 13. My sister went back to Cincinnati; the kids went on about their life, work, or school. Friends stopped coming to visit, and I was at home alone. It's strange how quiet a house can get; it was as if it too was mourning the loss of Mary Ann. Everywhere, in every room were reminders of her, bits of her life that told me that she had been there. Prayer shawls in several rooms, her slippers in the living room next to the chair she liked to sit in to watch the birds through the front window, pill bottles in the kitchen, bathroom and bedroom. All seemed to say she was still there, but she was gone. In the bedroom, her clothes, her perfume, even her shower items, all still spoke about her—all said she was there, but she was not. The worst was all the photographs all around the house showing a smiling Mary Ann with a family member. All seemed to stare at me as I passed them.

❧

The quietness of the house sometimes became overpowering. Small sounds that I didn't hear before seemed almost deafening, such as ice cubes falling into the tray, the tick of the grandfather clock, even the start-up of the air conditioner all seemed so much louder because they exemplified the emptiness of the house. All of it was depressing to me. I wondered from room to room, not able to stay in any one room very long. Even the dogs were silent, and I noticed that Rommel was still waiting for her to come home, still going to her bedroom to guard it, still walking around the bed to see if she was there. Harry just lay on the floor with his head between his paws. He was visibly depressed. Every now and again, he would come over by me while I sat in her La-Z-Boy and put his paw on my knee, as if to ask me where she was and also tell me it would be okay.

※

It is remarkable how slow time seems to go when you are alone. You start to wonder if anyone will call or come over, or if anyone still cares. I think about her every second of the day, replaying her struggle with cancer and wondering, if only I had done something different, if only I got her to go to another treatment facility, if only she had gotten tests for cancer before the diagnosis, if only, if only. I had an overwhelming sense of failure. I felt that I failed her when she needed me most. It played over and over in my head, and always the same question. Could I have saved her if I did something differently? Why did she have to die? The quietness and emptiness of the house magnified these thoughts, fed these emotions, and drove me deeper into the abyss of depression. I couldn't get these feelings out of my head. I had let the one I loved so much down. I continued to cry. I cried at seeing her picture, seeing some article of clothing, seeing a note she wrote to remind herself to take some medicine at some specific time. Almost anything made me break down and deepened the depression I was in.

❧

I could not get over her not ever coming home again. I felt like the male goose whose partner had just been killed, standing in quiet solitude on the edge of a lake, waiting for her to return. All her things were here. It was only natural to think she would come home, but I knew she never would. There would be no Mary Ann to talk to in the morning, or anytime. We would not share a meal again, and she would not lie next to me at night. I was alone, alone for the rest of my life.

Until the Twelfth
of Never

One of the things I thought about was how I could preserve Mary Ann's name at the school she taught at for twenty years. I knew the staff would remember her, and some students would too; but they would move on to high school and college, and she will be a distant memory. I want her memory to remain at the school she loved so much. I decided that the best way was to set up a scholarship in her name. I felt that since she taught English and religion, I would set up a scholarship for both of these. After talking to several teachers and the principal, I decided that it would only be a religion scholarship as the school already gave out an English scholarship.

❧

I talked to the teachers about the criteria for the scholarship, and we decided on several. The graduating eighth grader must attend a Catholic high school, must be active in the church, must perform community service, and must write a theme-based paper. I wanted the teachers to decide who the scholarship went to as they knew the kids. I also did not want the theme to be the deciding factor as some kids write better than others. The teachers agreed to a weighted system and they would have the last word. I also asked them to make sure that kids from financially disadvantaged homes were given greater consideration. Mary Ann always taught to help the disadvantaged and I wanted her scholarship to reflect that.

❧

I held several phone conferences with teachers and met with them once to finalize the scholarship. They announced the Mary Ann Simon Religion Scholarship in early October. I funded it, along with donations that people gave after we announced it at the funeral. Every year, one of the graduating eighth graders will receive a $1,000 scholarship in her name.

❧

After the funeral, I decided to write a book about Mary Ann's journey with cancer. I needed to start to work on it quickly as I didn't want to forget anything. I wrote *Losing You* from late July to the end of August. Now I realize that I would not have forgotten anything. It is all burned into my memory. Should the book sell, I will donate a significant part of the royalties to Pancreatic Cancer Research in her name. I will do everything I can to help eliminate this disease that took her life and so many others. I am hopeful that *Losing You* will help me do that.

❧

A Johnny Mathis song said, "You ask how long I'll need you, must I explain / I'll need you oh my darling like roses need rain." Throughout my life with Mary Ann, I told her that I loved her several times a day—in the morning before we left for work, when I came home, and especially at night when we went to bed. Sometimes she would reply just by saying "Bud," the nickname she gave to me early in our relationship. When she said that, I knew it was her way of saying "I love you." Many times, though, she would say, "Oh, you just think you do." "Well," I would say, "I do love you." Most people who knew her did not know that Mary Ann never considered herself to be even pretty or that someone would love her. She always rejected any statements that I made that she was beautiful and would tell me that I needed glasses.

❧

She could not understand why anyone would love her. I thought that she was the most beautiful girl I had ever seen; so it was natural for her not to believe me when I told her that I loved her or that she was beautiful and because of this I had to tell her all the time that I loved her every day of my life. Even if we had a fight, I would tell her that I loved her and always would. I made it a point that if we had a fight, I would apologize before we went to bed even if it was her fault. You see, there was nothing more important in my life than her. We never went to bed mad at each other. She would sometimes ask, "And how long is that?" that I would love her. "Until the twelfth of never," I would reply, which was a line from a Johnny Mathis song that we both liked. "Until the twelfth of never / and that's a long, long time."

The Visitations

When I am home in Cleveland, I go and visit with Mary Ann every day, as I had promised I would the day of the funeral, when I was alone with her I promised her I would come to visit with her every day I am home. I promised that I would be there in any weather, that I loved her and would not ever forget her. Before the monument was ready, my son Greg made a cross with her name on it to make it easier for others to find her. I would never forget where she is.

❧

I usually come in the morning to see her. I bring the shower seat I got for her the last couple of months she was alive because I was afraid she would fall in the shower. I sit on the seat next to her grave so that I can see the headstone and she can see me. I make sure that she has fresh flowers when I come to see her. I talk to her about everything. I know she is worrying about the finances, as she always did, but I always tell her that everything is all right. She never knew that we owed all the bills from 2011 as we were forced out of network because the clinic would not treat her. In 2012, I changed the coverage so that out-of-network bills were paid, but only at 60%. We owed hundreds of thousands in medical bills.

❧

I tell her not to worry, that all is okay. I don't want her to worry about such things. I told her about the changes to the house, the wood floors and countertop, and later the new refrigerator, the stove, and the microwave. I want her to be happy with the changes. These are things we talked about for a long time, but she would never let me spend the money to have them done even though we had saved for them and had the money in the bank. She hated spending money even when she wanted or needed things. That set me up as the "spender" because I knew she wanted or needed something but would not buy it for herself. She always worried about money even though I made a very good salary and she really didn't have to work if she didn't want to. After all, she didn't work for almost twelve years when we had our family and I made much less money then. I tell her about Sara, Mike, and Ava and bring pictures to show her. I know she can see them. I tell her about all the kids and what is new in their life. One topic was Greg and Amy's new baby, Joey, whom she never got to see. I always tell her about work and all the things I am doing. She always asked about it each time we talked on the phone. I'd give anything to talk to her on the phone now.

I always pray for her when I visit. I ask how she is doing and hope that she is happy; who couldn't be happy in heaven? I ask that she wait for me. I want to be with her forever and I am afraid that she will not remember me. I spend a lot of time reminiscing about our life together and how happy I was. I always tell her that she made me the luckiest man alive and I hope that I made her happy.

One day in June 2012, we were sitting together on the glider on the patio, she had been silent for a while when she looked at me and said, "I think we had a good life together, don't you?" This told me that she was thinking about her death and assessing our life together. She wanted reassurance that I was happy with her, that I loved her. I told her "I thought we had a wonderful life together, one that I would never change." I told her that "I still can't believe that I was lucky enough to have married you" and that "I am looking forward to many more years together." I gave her a big hug and a kiss and told her that "You are my one and only love and I will love you to the end of time." She laid her head on my shoulder, wrapped her hand around mine and said, "I hope so."

The marker looks beautiful, and with the addition of the grass that was planted and started growing in October, it looks even better. There is a flower holder next to the stone that I fill with fresh flowers every time I come to see her. The first time I put flowers in the holder, they were gone the next morning. I saw that they were eaten down as far as they could be by deer. I found their foot tracks around the grave. I put silk flowers in the holder in the winter as they never fade and deer won't eat them. She will always have flowers. I have asked Sara to make sure she has them when I am in Louisiana.

I promised Mary Ann I would visit every day I am home, and I have kept that promise. I have visited her during some very hot weather, in driving rain, and in snow eight inches deep, where I had to find her and clear away the snow. As I always tell her, I will be there every day I am home. I will come because I love her. I will never forget her, and one day, in God's good time, I will lie there with her, never to leave her again.

The Journey Back

When I am in Cleveland, I am alone much of the time. I do see the kids, and I have the dogs, but the nights are the loneliest. Back in Louisiana, it is much worse. During the weekdays, I am at work, but each night, I go to an empty house. There is no one there, ever, except me. I hear from the kids sporadically. Sara calls or sends e-mails irregularly. Matt never calls me in the evening. Greg almost never calls at all. I hear from Becky about every ten days. There have been times when I don't talk to anyone for two weeks. I do not call them as I do not want to bother them. Mary Ann and I always felt it is the kids' responsibility to call their parents. She never, or only rarely, called Sara or Becky just to chat.

꙳

I do not feel like doing anything when I'm in Louisiana, and that includes cooking. There are many nights that I heat up a can of peas or green beans for supper. I just have no desire to make anything. I used to call her every night and talk even if it was about nothing. Just to hear her voice was enough for me to keep my spirits up. Now there is nothing but emptiness and silence. I sometimes call our house phone as she recorded the greeting just to hear her voice again I'd give anything to talk to her on the phone again. I remember the plane trip back from Cleveland the first time I went back after the funeral. The two and a half hour trip seemed like it took a year. All the way all I thought about was her and the fight she put up against the cancer. I thought about how she cried just before she died. I truly believe that she wanted to say I love you but could not talk.

⚘

Weekends in Louisiana are the worst. I get up every day at 5:00 a.m. and have to be alone until I go to bed about 11:00 p.m. Most weekends, no one calls. I look at my phone from time to time, hoping that I will see a missed-call message, but most of the time, there are no calls. I clean the house and wash clothes, but how much wash or how dirty can the house get with one person? All this time on my hands leads me to think about Mary Ann and what happened to her. I talk to her in the darkness of the house and wish for a response, but there is nothing.

⚘

This is my life, alone with my thoughts, with my images of her in my mind. This is not living; but it is reality now, and I can only hope that I will be able to join her soon. I talk to her every day and night. In the silence of the house, I hear strains of "The Sounds of Silence," "Hello darkness my old friend, / I've come to talk with you again"

The Christmas Bell

Christmastime was always one of our favorite times of the year. We loved seeing all the houses decorated in beautiful light displays. We were always excited to get our tree up, along with all of the decorations throughout the house. Mary Ann always started baking Christmas cookies several weeks before Christmas. The smell of those cookies seemed to keep the house smelling good all season. Of course, we always hoped for snow for Christmas.

※

I liked this time of the year because I could buy pretty much what I wanted for Mary Ann, and I usually did. I think that I averaged three or four hundred dollars just in clothes for her at Christmas. She would never buy anything she needed, so that left the matter to me, and I always bought her the best. I remember one year I got her over three hundred dollars' worth of Victoria's Secret. She claimed she was embarrassed, but I knew she was not; and in fact, she loved what I picked out. She would not tell people the truth about what I had gotten her for

Christmas that year; she just said clothes. Every year, I bought her the newest products from Estée Lauder, her favorite perfume company. She had every perfume, cologne, dusting powder set—every product they had made in the last twenty years. She always told me that I overdid it, but I knew better. I got what I wanted for the one I was so in love with.

※

We had so many decorations in the house it was hard to put them all out, so we kept some put away and rotated them with others so the house didn't look cluttered. One reason for this was that every Christmas, on the last day of school, her classes would give her presents. Many of those were some kind of ornament or music box or some other decoration. She kept them all and always wrote thank-you notes to her students.

※

We did have many music boxes and musical snow globes, but the one that she liked the best wasn't one of the Hummel's or snow-globes it was a music box that cost twenty five cents that Matt had gotten for her at the Christmas store at school when he was in the fourth grade. This music box was shaped like a school bell, which she really liked, and the handle was Santa. It played "Santa Claus Is Coming to Town" and the Santa turned as the music played. That was at least twenty-three years ago. At Christmas she kept the bell on top of the piano next to a wooden schoolhouse. Over the years, Santa stopped turning. No one remembers when exactly that was, but all agree it was some time ago. Even though Santa did not turn, the music still played. When we put the music boxes away for the year, we play them out as it might damage the spring to let them sit with the springs wound.

This year was the first Christmas since Mary Ann had died and Sara came over and put all the decorations out, just like her mother would have wanted. The school bell was placed on the piano next to the schoolhouse as she always had placed it. All the music boxes were unwound just as they were when we put them away the year before. A while later, Matt came home from work, and he and Sara were sitting at the kitchen table talking when they heard the music playing from the living room. It was "Santa Claus Is Coming to Town." They went into the living room; and sure enough, the bell was playing loud and clear. She and Matt went into the living room and after all the years of standing still, Santa had started turning again. Sara said the bell was not wound when she took it from its box and that both she and Matt remembered that Santa had not turned for years but was turning again. They both thought Mom had been there. She wanted to hear her favorite music box again.

※

They let it play out, and both thought that Mary Ann wanted to hear it one more time. When Sara came the next day to finish with the decorations, she wound the bell, but Santa did not turn; and throughout the holiday season, whenever the bell was played, Santa would stand motionless.

※

Merry Christmas, honey. We love and miss you so.

Memories of Home

I was just thinking the other night about my memories of Mary Ann and her home before we married. I remembered that her mother was a great cook. The first time I ate at their house, it was a supper during the week. Her father usually got home just after 6:00 p.m. and always gave the socks he wore that day at his job to their dog who would carry them into the bathroom and drop them on the floor. The meal was pork chops, mashed potatoes, some vegetable, a salad, and milk to drink, except for her father, who always had coffee. I remember that her mother always served everyone before she sat down to eat. This, I learned, was a Polish tradition. As I said, her mother was a great cook, but she never taught Mary Ann. In fact, when she was cooking, Mary Ann was rarely allowed in the kitchen to help. Although this allowed us to spend more time together, it also meant that when we did get married Mary Ann knew very little about cooking but she became a very good cook.

Even so, I never once told her that I didn't like what she made. Well, except once, it was the salmon patty affair. I like salmon, and so did the kids, but there was something that she did to it that made it impossible to eat. I remember the kids and I were sitting at the kitchen table when she brought out the infamous patties. More properly called hockey pucks, they were round, almost three inches in diameter, about one inch high and as hard as rocks. I had asked her before not to make them again as no one liked them. She must have thought that if she changed the recipe, we would like them. I'm afraid the result was the same. Hockey pucks! I picked up the plate and threw them on the plate in the sink. I think she was shocked, but everyone else was happy they didn't have to try to eat them. We ordered pizza, and she never made them again.

※

The Christmas tree affair was a classic. Her father always bought his tree from the same dealer every Christmas, but I convinced him that a fresh-cut tree is much better as it is not cut down in August like many of the trees that dealers sell. It is also not spray-painted green to hide the browning needles. He reluctantly agreed, and Mary Ann and I set out to find the perfect tree. It was much like the scene from *Christmas Vacation*, where Clark Griswold takes the family to find his perfect tree. I asked her to stay in the car as it was cold and snowing and I didn't think I would be gone long. The place we went to was a Christmas tree farm that boasted of the largest selection in the area. Little did I realize that it also meant it was the largest acreage in the area. I left to look for the tree with a bow saw and street shoes in six-plus inches of snow and temperatures hovering in the low twenties. Only God knows what the wind chill was. After two hours and darkness about to settle in, Mary Ann decided that I had died of hypothermia and went to the owner to find the frozen body.

౿

Just as they came down the first aisle I was coming from the opposite end with the tree. I don't know how she could have doubted me. We got it just four days before Christmas, so it was as fresh as it could be. Her father always put it up Christmas Eve and then took it down the day after the New Year. The tree was up only eleven days, but before New Year's Eve, there wasn't one needle left on it. All the needles were in a circular pattern on the ground around the tree. What was worse, each day we could hear the tinkle of needles as they fell off the tree, hitting ornaments on the way to the ground. Truly, it was a Charlie Brown Christmas tree. Her father never said much about it, though, except once in a while, he would say, "There's a lot to be said for fresh trees"—an obvious dig at Mary Ann and me.

These are some of the memories I have of our courtship, of her family life, and of a time long ago.

The Debt

I had taken over the bills when I got home shortly before Mary Ann died. I consolidated all the savings accounts and put almost all the bills on automatic pay so that I did not have to remember all of them to pay. I also paid off most of the store charges, which eliminated monthly payments for cards I would never use. This left only the medical bills from her treatment that I had to deal with.

❧

All the bills from May 2011 through the end of December 2011 were not covered by insurance. We were forced out of the network when the clinic refused to treat Mary Ann. Our coverage would not pay out of network if in-network facilities were available. In fact, they were available; they just would not treat her. During this time, we incurred well over $600,000 in charges from hospitals that provided chemo treatment and several hundred thousand dollars for in-hospital confinements, the treating doctor, and the home health nurses who came to our house every time she had chemo to remove the chemo pack (which she called her ghost buster pack), plus all the ancillary services that she used. Just to give an example: it cost over $5,000 every time they disconnected her from the pack, and this occurred two or three times a month. In order to pay these bills, I started to empty savings accounts that were intended for retirement. I started to get collection calls on my cell phone, which I did not answer.

※

By January 2012, we were covered for out of network because I changed the insurance program. However, only 60 percent of the bills were covered, after the deductible was met, which meant I owed the yearly deductable plus 40 percent. This was better, but the treatment costs increased in 2012 because she needed different drugs, and she went on radiation therapy. All of this drained our retirement savings and did not pay off all the bills. Mary Ann never knew anything about the medical bill situation because she had enough to worry about; and as her cancer progressed, she just wasn't well enough to discuss it. I wanted to shield her from this aspect of her struggle; and if she asked, I told her that the insurance was taking care of the bills. The bills totaled almost $1 million for 2011 and 2012.

※

Once I came back to Louisiana, I started to file the bills and keep closer track of what the insurance company paid. This was an eye-opener by itself. I was surprised by all the bills that were initially denied due to some clerical error from the provider. I had to contact the provider and request that they change whatever had been identified as an error. It seemed to me that the providers were more willing to request that I pay the entire amount instead of simply correcting their error. A perfect example of insurance denials was the bills from the hospital stay in South Carolina. All these bills, all $56,000, were initially denied by my carrier; and it took several phone calls to different departments to get them to reconsider the bill, which was eventually covered at 60 percent.

❧

These bills occupy my time on weekends while I am alone in Louisiana. I do not know when all the bills are going to be paid off, and I do not know when I will get a final accounting from the insurance companies. What I do know is that I will not be retiring anytime soon. So, besides the fact that I have lost my wife, I am left with the task of repaying these bills and the prospect of not ever being able to retire. I do not think that the system is fair or equitable. It seems to me that if the treatment had been successful, I would not have any problem paying the bills, as they would have represented a life-saving treatment. However, the fact is that medical science failed my wife and my family. I lost my wife and my children lost their mother. Perhaps they should consider accepting what the insurance companies paid as full payment for an unsuccessful effort. All of this is a heavy burden on someone who has just lost someone who was everything to him. It weighs you down, makes you physically ill, and sends you deeper into depression.

Happy Birthday, Baby

Mary Ann was born on September 11, 1951. This chapter is out of order, simply because I did not want to deal with it. On her birthday in 2012, she had been dead for two months and four days. The memories of her death were too fresh in my mind for me to deal with a birthday that was never to be. For me, it was too painful, too soon after her loss for me to cope with a birthday that I could not ever celebrate again. Not this year, not anymore.

❦

I always tried to make her birthday special. If it fell during the week, I would send flowers to school. She was always excited to receive them there, as were her students, who always asked what the note that was sent with the flowers said. I always took this occasion to buy her clothes or jewelry, and sometimes both, but always the best. I never looked at prices, as nothing was too good for her. She would sometimes get upset with me, because as she said, she knew what I had paid for some item. I would always tell her, "You are worth the world to me. So don't look at the cost."

※

Sometimes if her birthday fell during the week, I would come home early and make dinner for her. She loved lobster, and I would buy her a whole one that I usually had to break open for her. Of course, she had drawn butter with it. The dinner would include a vegetable, usually broccoli, her favorite, and a baked potato with the works on it, bacon, butter, cheese, and sour cream. I always got her a birthday cake from the Italian bakery in our neighborhood. It was a layered cake with fruit and a chocolate cream layer that I knew she loved.

※

If her birthday fell on a weekend, I took her out to one of her favorite restaurants. She picked it, and I made the reservations. I would always get her a birthday card that said all the things I felt for her. I always signed the card and the flower cards "Bud," her pet name for me. The first time one of her students saw the card and read the name *Bud*, she wanted to know who he was. She would laugh and say, "He's my boyfriend."

※

I was her boyfriend and her lover and her husband. Her birthday meant more to me than I think it did to her. It was a day when I could do the things for her that I knew meant something to her, that comforted her, that made her feel loved and wanted and it made her feel special, because she was special to me. Throughout the forty-plus years that I've known her, I made sure that her day was special. I wanted her to know that she was loved, was needed, and was appreciated for all the things that she did for all of us during the year. I made sure that the kids all made a card for her, and I bought a present that they gave to her just from them. For me, that was a chance to get her more presents, so I was a little disappointed when they started to buy her things on their own. She always knew that I bought their presents, and she did the same thing on my birthday and I got presents from Harry. She loved to give Harry a cookie and tell him to "take it to Daddy," and he would come trotting happily over to me, but the cookie was always gone by the time he got to me. Harry could never figure out what happened, but we knew and had great fun watching him try to find the cookie she gave him. I do think that the presents that they bought were more meaningful than mine just because they picked them out and paid for them themselves. I remember that they couldn't wait for her birthday to arrive so the boys would keep giving her hints about what their present was, and she would almost always guess before the day arrived.

❧

My two favorite days of the year, Christmas and her birthday, were now more or less meaningless. She was gone, and all I had were the memories of birthdays gone by, of the happiness I saw in her face, the twinkle in her eyes as she opened the presents—all was gone now but for the memories that still live on in my mind. I remember how happy I was that I could brighten her day and make her realize how loved she was by me, her family, and by her friends.

Happy birthday, baby.

The Wee, Small Hours of the Morning

Frank Sinatra sang a song titled "The Wee Small Hours of the Morning" that said, "In the wee small hours of the morning, when the whole wide world is fast asleep / You lie awake and you think about the girl and never ever think of counting sheep." I identify with this song; I know what it is all about. Since she died, I can count on one hand the number of good night's sleep I have had. Always it's the same. I go to bed about eleven, or when I find myself starting to doze on the couch. With almost-military precision, I awake about two fifteen in the morning with her on my mind.

❧

Every night I awake with different thoughts of her. It could be some aspect of the treatment, some memory of things we did or places we went, memories of her. I wonder why I am thinking about this now and then I lie awake thinking about her and trying to relive our life together. I finally get up about 3:00 a.m. and sit in the living room looking at pictures of her and going over in my head her journey with cancer and wondering why she had to die, and what, if anything, I could have or should have done to save her and why she had to leave me. It was during one of these nights that I realized I had failed her when she needed me the most. I couldn't save her, couldn't take the pain away, couldn't stop the sickness she felt most of the time, couldn't stop the progression of the cancer, couldn't stop the weight loss couldn't help the one I loved so much no matter how much I begged God to let me take her place. I failed her and I will leave this life a failure.

The song goes on to say, "When your lonely heart has learned its lesson…" I guess my lonely heart has not learned its lesson. She is on my mind constantly, always, even when I sleep. I can't conceive of a time I will not have her on my mind. I want her on my mind. It is the only way I have to keep a hold of her, to keep her present in my life.

Each night, in the wee small hours, she comes to me again. I tell her how much I love her, how much I miss her, how sorry I am. As the song says, "In the wee small hours of the morning,/that's the time you miss her most of all."

Till There Was You

As I think back on my life with Mary Ann, I realize that I am a better person for having known her. Mary Ann was always there to be a sounding board for me and as my guide while I made my way through rough waters. One of her many accomplishments in life was to bring a fallen-away Catholic back to the church. Her faith was strong even before she ever taught school. Once we started to date steadily, I went to church with her almost every Sunday. She always said, "You don't have to go if you don't want to." But I did want to go—at first just to be with her, later, my faith reemerged. She must have been praying hard for me.

❧

She encouraged me when I started my career and always made the bumps in my road seem trivial. I cannot tell you how much her support meant to me. She built up my confidence at some low points in my life and kept me focused on the future. As I said earlier, I fell in love with her the first night we met. I told her on the second date that I loved her and was going to marry her. She said anxiously, "Wait a minute, I haven't agreed to anything." I told her, "I know, but you will." Mary Ann had a hard time accepting the fact that she was beautiful and that someone would want to love and marry her. I may not have been sure of many things at that point in my life, but I was sure that I loved her more than anything in my life, and over the years, my love for her would only grow.

❧

I can honestly say that before I met her, I had never felt love for anyone else beyond my family, but that was a different kind of love. *If there was a theme for our life together, it was love.* Love for her became central to my life with her. Everything I did was because I loved her so much. After the first year we were together, she told me she loved me. Now when the woman you are in love with tells you she loves you, it just increases the intensity of your love. Such was our case.

❧

I remember near the end of her life she told me that she couldn't believe that I was doing things to help her that she couldn't do herself. I looked her in the eyes and said, "Honey, why would you ever question what I do? I do these things because I love you." I reminded her that our vows said "in sickness and in health." I was determined to be there for her. She would just shake her head and say, "I guess you really do." I think that it was during this period that she finally realized and accepted the fact that I did love her. In fact, there was nothing I wouldn't do for her. If it is possible, my love for her deepened during her journey with cancer as did, I think, her love for me.

🌿

Hindsight is always twenty-twenty and as I look back on our relationship, I realize what a huge part in my life our love for each other played. Throughout our lives together, Mary Ann was not as vocal about stating her love for me as I was with my love for her; whereas I told her I loved her almost constantly. She did things that showed me her love, and even if she didn't say "I love you" back every time, she would look at me and just say, "Bud,"… and I knew. That I knew was all I ever wanted. When I look back on our life, I realize how strong a bond we did form, how much we loved each other regardless of any occasional disagreements.

🌿

There are no perfect couples, but if you truly love the person you married you swallow your pride and make the marriage work. You do that because there is no one on earth more important to you than the one you married, the one you love and because you swore an oath to God that you would love, honor and cherish the other person. There was nothing in this world that meant more to me than Mary Ann. I didn't care if she ever acknowledged fault, I would, because I loved her more than anything in my life. She was more important to me than my personal pride. I love you Mary Ann, from the first moment I saw you, I loved you and will till the last breath I take. I loved you Mary Ann—then, now, and forever. You completed me, made my life whole and worth living, enriched my soul. You are gone now, but I will always love you. There's a song that says, "There was love all around, but I never heard it singing,/ no I never heard it at all, *Till there was you.*"

Epilogue

When the person you spent your life loving and caring for dies, you understandably feel an overwhelming sense of loss. This grief takes over your life, and you wonder how you will be able to go on without them. I have felt this depression, this grief ever since Mary Ann passed. I know that I will never in this world touch her, kiss her, hold her again. *But I have come to understand that the most important aspect of our relationship is still there and, for that matter, always would be there, our love for each other. It will never die.*

☙

Time passes, and I am without her. But I still have her, still have my love for her. I know that she still loves me and that someday we will be together again for eternity. No matter how long I may live, I will miss her, but I will never stop loving her. I will always think back on our life and think only of the good times and remember how much I loved her and how much she loved me.

☙

I promise you, Mary Ann that I will never think of myself as being without you again. *I will never be without you again, Mary Ann, because I love you, and love is eternal.*

Postscript

Mary Ann's ninety-three-year-old mother passed away in February 2013. Personally, I think that losing her only daughter was too much for her to bear. She is now seven plots away from Mary Ann and next to her husband. In a short time I lost a family.